DON'T RUN

Verlag der Buchhandlung
Walther und Franz König, Köln

Wabi Sabi (2000)

Wabi (2000)

"ZA-patos" poster (1981)

Due to copyright, the image on this spread cannot be shown. Please read the description.

This is a photo of a man in a military uniform marching, his right foot is in mid-air and his left foot is on the ground. He seems to be in a parade or a training march as his uniform is similar to what military soldiers wear. The man is wearing black shoes. The background is a blurry gray colored street. This particular picture was probably taken at a parade or ceremony.

Image description generated by ChatGPT.

Camper Together with 99%IS (2015)

Pix BCN (2023)

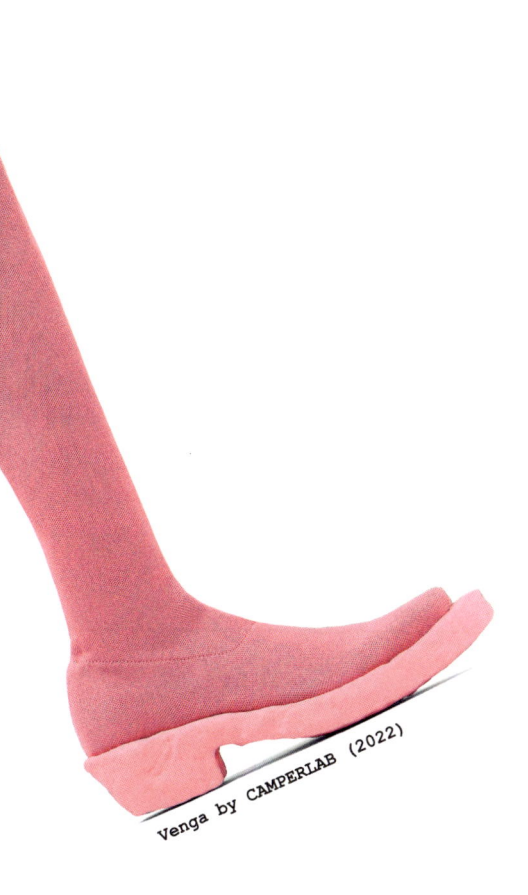
Venga by CAMPERLAB (2022)

Pelotas Ariel (1995)

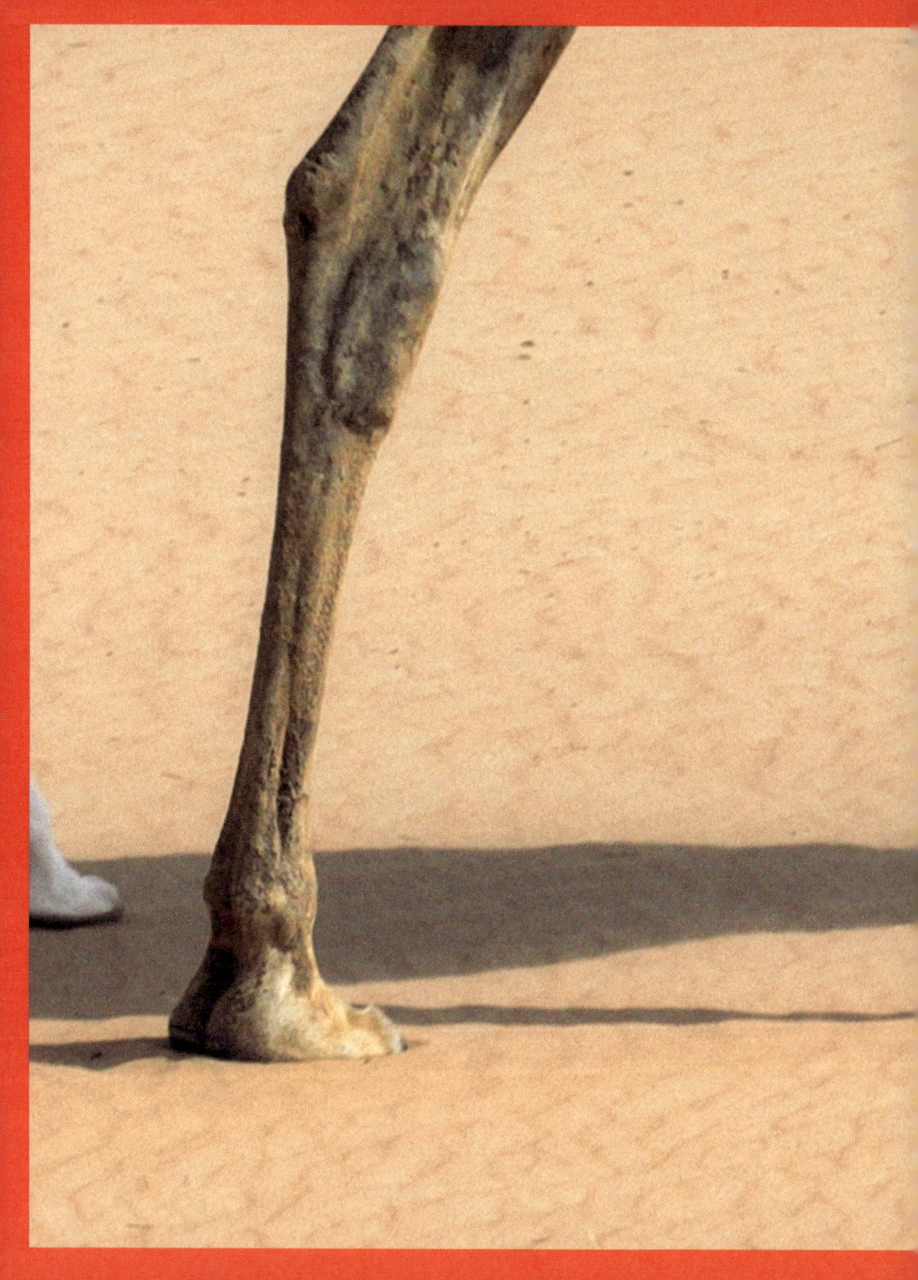

Wabi Sombrilla (2000)

ABS (2019)

Hastalavista by CAMPERLAB (2020)

Pelotas (1995)

50 YEARS YOUNG

The year is 2025 and Camper is 50. Back in 1975, Lorenzo Fluxa, my father, founded a brand that was born to be unique, building on a family shoemaking company created by my great-grandfather Antonio Fluxa in 1877 in Inca, Mallorca. To a shoemaking heritage rooted in quality and craftsmanship, my father added design and comfort to create a different brand with a new perspective. Today, 50 years on, we are still passionate about preserving our uniqueness by designing exceptional products of the highest quality with the greatest respect for our environment.

What better way to mark our 50th birthday than with a visual history of our brand. We are shoemakers, but Camper is so much more than that: it's a whole world of creativity, from our campaigns to our store designs. But we are shoemakers. So we decided that the best way to tell our story was through our shoes: let *them* do the talking. These pages look back at our collections over the past five decades, in no particular order, to celebrate the imagination, diversity, and eclecticism of Camper so far.

I cannot end without thanking everyone who has made this journey possible. So many people across different generations have made Camper what it is today. It is an honor to celebrate this anniversary when the brand is stronger than ever, with great products, a strong connection to younger generations, and our fantastic team.

Here's to the next half-century and the next chapter.

Miguel Fluxa

Eki by CAMPERLAB (2021)

Katie (2018)

Pelotas XLite (2017)

Pelotas Ariel (1995)

Pelotas for Kids (1995)

Wabi (2000)

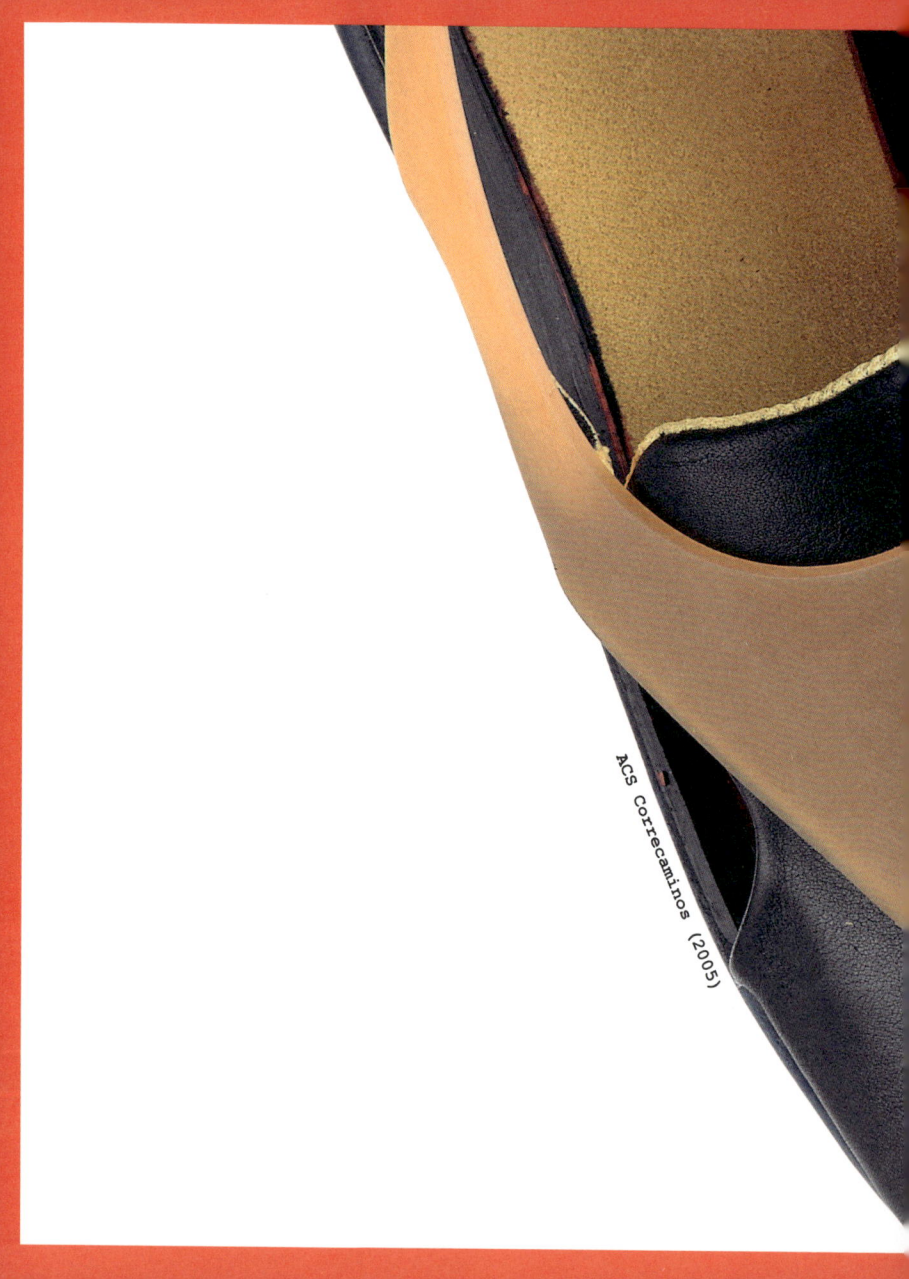

ACS Correcaminos (2005)

Hipopotamus (1991)

TWINS for Kids (1988)

TWINS (1988)

Match (2013)

ke (1990)

Katie (2019)

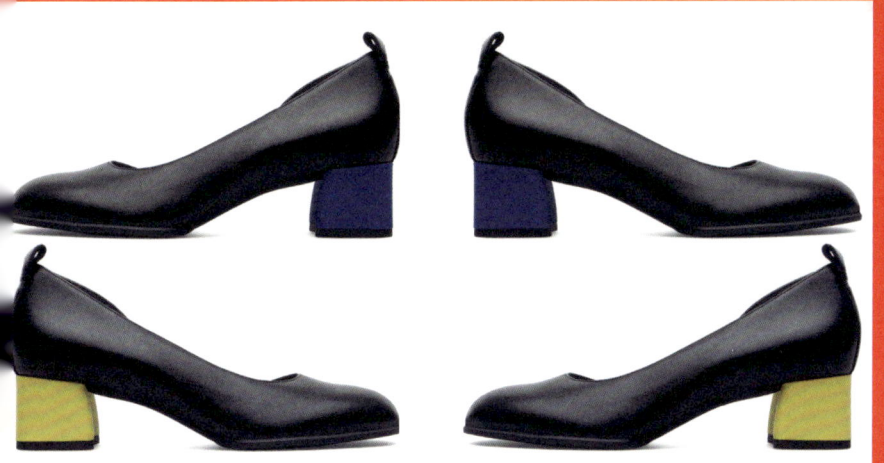

This is a black-and-white photograph of a classic boxing match. The two boxers are engaged in close-range combat, with one fighter throwing a punch as the other prepares to block or counter. The boxer on the left appears to be taking or anticipating a hit, while the boxer on the right leans in with a determined look. Both fighters are wearing traditional boxing gloves and trunks, with the "Everlast" brand visible on their gear.

The setting appears to be a boxing ring under bright overhead lights, illuminating the fighters' muscular physiques and capturing the intensity of the moment. The composition of the photograph emphasizes the struggle, strategy, and physical effort in boxing. The image likely captures a historic or well-known match due to the classic appearance and black-and-white format.

Image description generated by ChatGPT.

Pelotas Ariel (1995)

TWINS (1988)

TWINS (1988)

This image captures a powerful scene of a protest or rally. A large group of people, mostly young adults and children, are assembled in the middle of a street, holding protest signs and banners.

The signs and banners
The signs display diverse messages, all expressing a plea for justice. Some prominent signs read:

"We are Praying With Our Feet," emphasizing their unwavering commitment. "Blow Your Horn In Memory of Mike & Brown," highlighting the tragic loss of lives. "Hands Up," a powerful phrase demanding accountability. "We Are The Victims." This sign underscores the shared experience of oppression.

The emotions are palpable
The young people are visibly passionate, their faces reflecting a mixture of anger, frustration, and determination. Some individuals, particularly the children, appear weary. Their expressions embody the weight of their struggles and their desire for change.

Due to copyright, the image on this spread cannot be shown. Please read the description.

A sense of community
The unity of the participants is evident as they stand together in solidarity. The shared purpose and the messages on the signs create a strong sense of community and shared cause.

The backdrop
The image's backdrop reveals a quintessential city setting, further highlighting the context of the protest. This setting suggests that the fight for justice is taking place in the heart of the community.

Overall, this image conveys a powerful message of hope and resilience. It captures the spirit of a community united in its demand for justice, equality, and a better future. The image raises awareness about the importance of peaceful protests and the essential need for social change.

Image description generated by ChatGPT.

Camaleón 1975 (2021)

Peu (prototype) (2010)

This image shows four people crossing a city street at a crosswalk, reminiscent of the famous "Abbey Road" photograph by The Beatles. The setting is urban, with modern buildings, parked cars, and a bright, sunny day with a few clouds in the sky.

Each individual has a distinct style and appears to be carrying photography or media equipment: The first person on the left is a man with a beard, wearing a checkered shirt and dark jeans, carrying a large tripod on his shoulder and a professional camera around his neck.

The second person, next to him, is dressed in a business-casual outfit with a white shirt, tie, and gray pants, holding a black bag, possibly a briefcase.

The third person, a woman with long red or blonde hair, is dressed casually in a light shirt and ripped jeans, carrying a shoulder bag and another bag across her body.

The fourth person, on the far right, has long blonde hair and is wearing a black patterned dress, carrying a portfolio or laptop case.

The group is walking across the street in a single file, each looking forward in a relaxed, purposeful stride. The image captures a sense of movement, contemporary style, and possibly a creative or professional group at work.

Image description generated by ChatGPT.

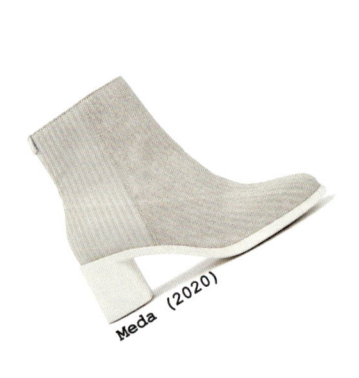

Meda (2020)

Slippers Sun (2016)

Uno (2013)

Due to copyright, the image on this spread cannot be shown. Please read the description.

The image shows a close-up of a performer on stage. He is wearing black dress pants with a gold stripe down the side, paired with shiny black shoes with white socks. The person also appears to be wearing a sequined black jacket and a single white glove. The image captures a dynamic moment, likely mid-dance or performance, with his foot lifted as if preparing for a move.

Image description generated by ChatGPT.

MIL 1978 by CAMPERLAB (2021)

Vintar (2014)

TWINS Camper Together with Isamaya Ffrench (2017)

Due to copyright, the image on this spread cannot be shown. Please read the description.

The image shows two Dalmatians sitting on a paved sidewalk. Both dogs have the distinctive white coats with black spots that Dalmatians are known for. The dog on the left has a red collar with a leash attached, while the dog on the right has a black collar with a more elaborate design and is also on a leash.

The dogs are sitting close to each other but are looking in slightly different directions. The background appears to be a stone wall and part of a dark green or black street post. Both dogs look calm, sitting in an alert posture, and appear well-behaved.

Image description generated by ChatGPT.

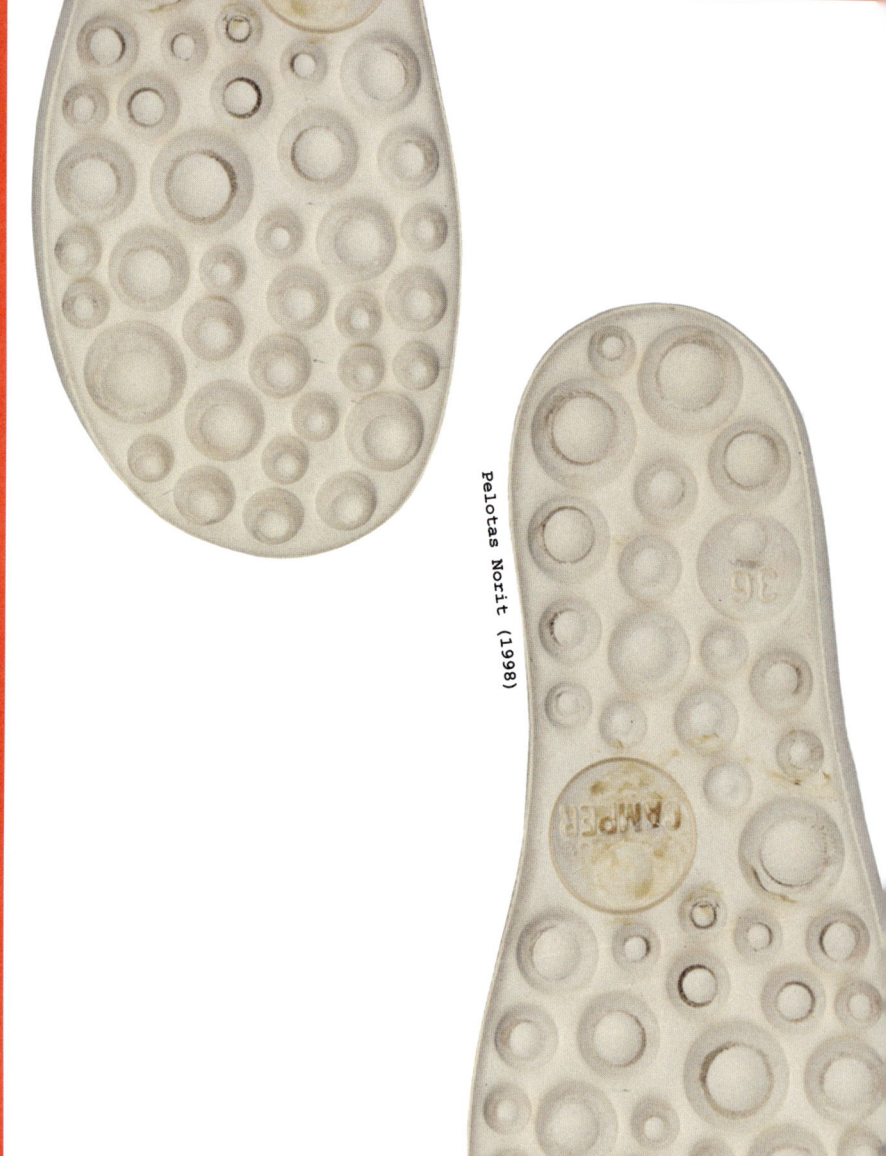

Pelotas Norit (1998)

Pelotas Ariel (1995)

Due to copyright, the image on this spread cannot be shown. Please read the description.

The image likely depicts the Pope, identifiable by the distinctive attire. The close-up shows bright red leather shoes, a traditional element often associated with papal dress, symbolizing humility and the blood of Christian martyrs. The Pope's shoes contrast with the white robe, adorned with intricate gold embroidery and tassels, adding an element of elegance and reverence to the ceremonial outfit. The white socks and low-heeled red shoes contribute to the papal look, emphasizing both tradition and symbolic significance in the Pope's attire during formal religious occasions.

Image description generated by ChatGPT.

Thelma (2017)

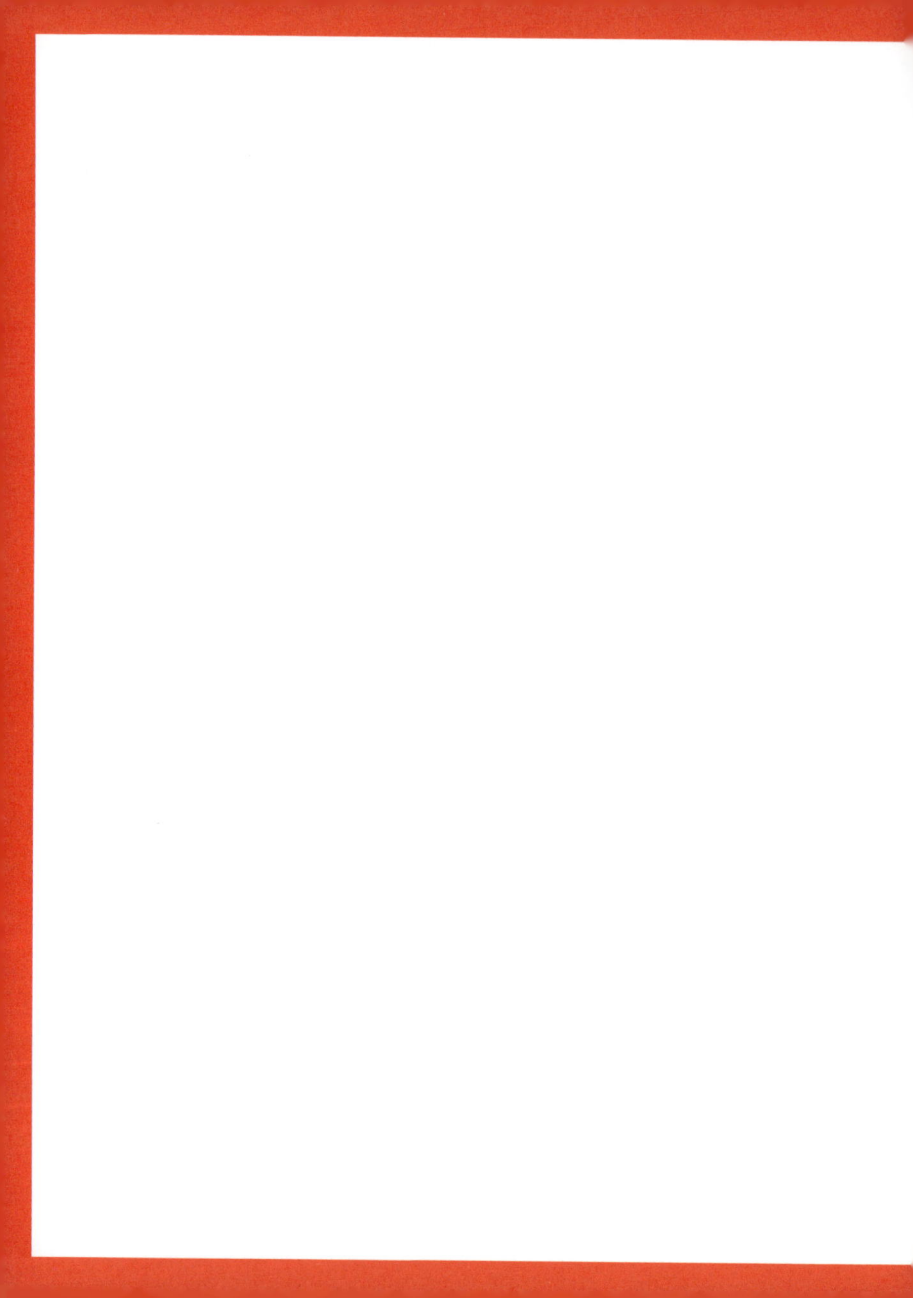

Terra (1994)

Traktori by CAMPERLAB (2023)

Teix (1997)

Terra & Camaleón (2001)

Peu Stadium (2021)

Wabi (2000)

Oruga Sandal (2014)

Peu Senda (2008)

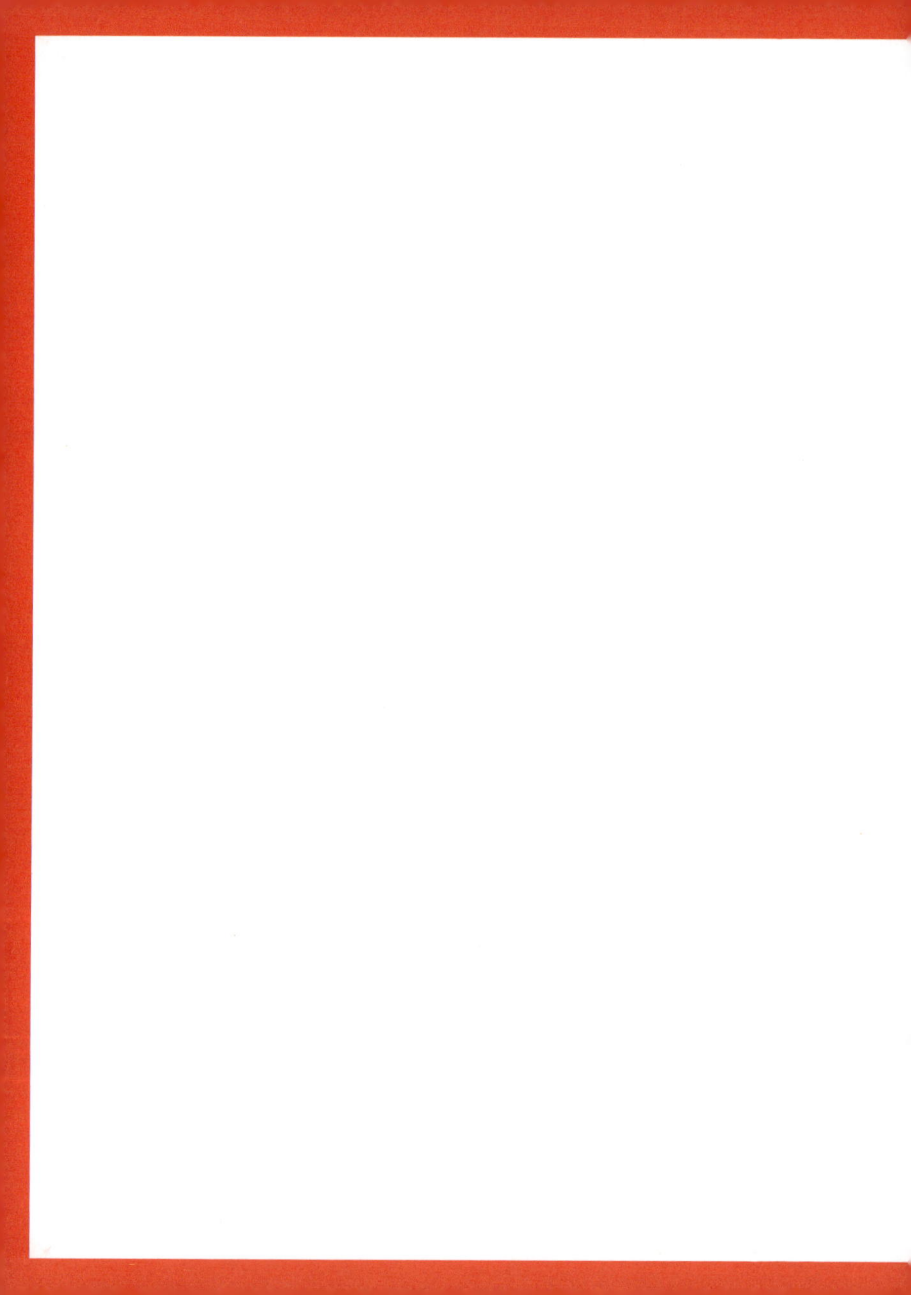

TWINS (1988)

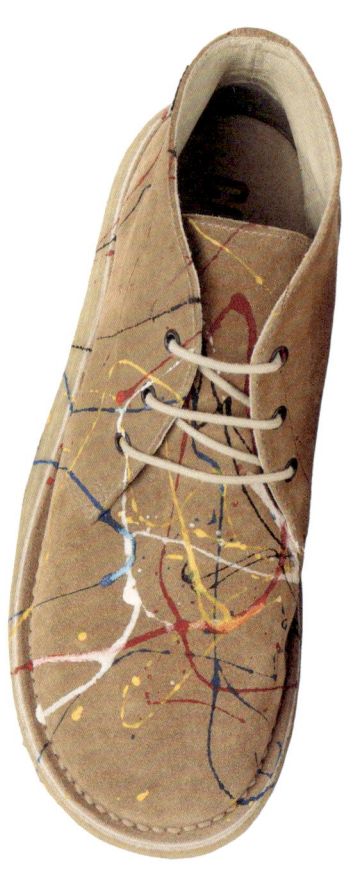

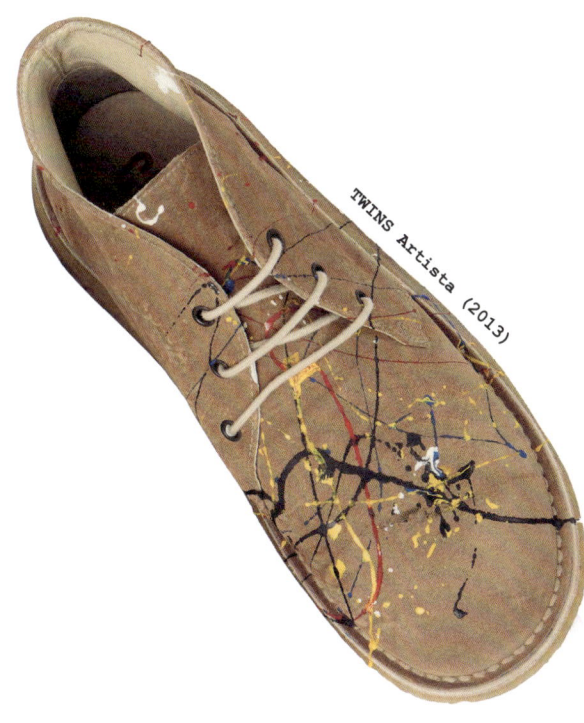

TWINS Artista (2013)

Aqua (2001)

Tormenta by CAMPERLAB (2023)

Terra (2001)

Tossu by CAMPERLAB (2022)

Tormenta by CAMPERLAB (2023)

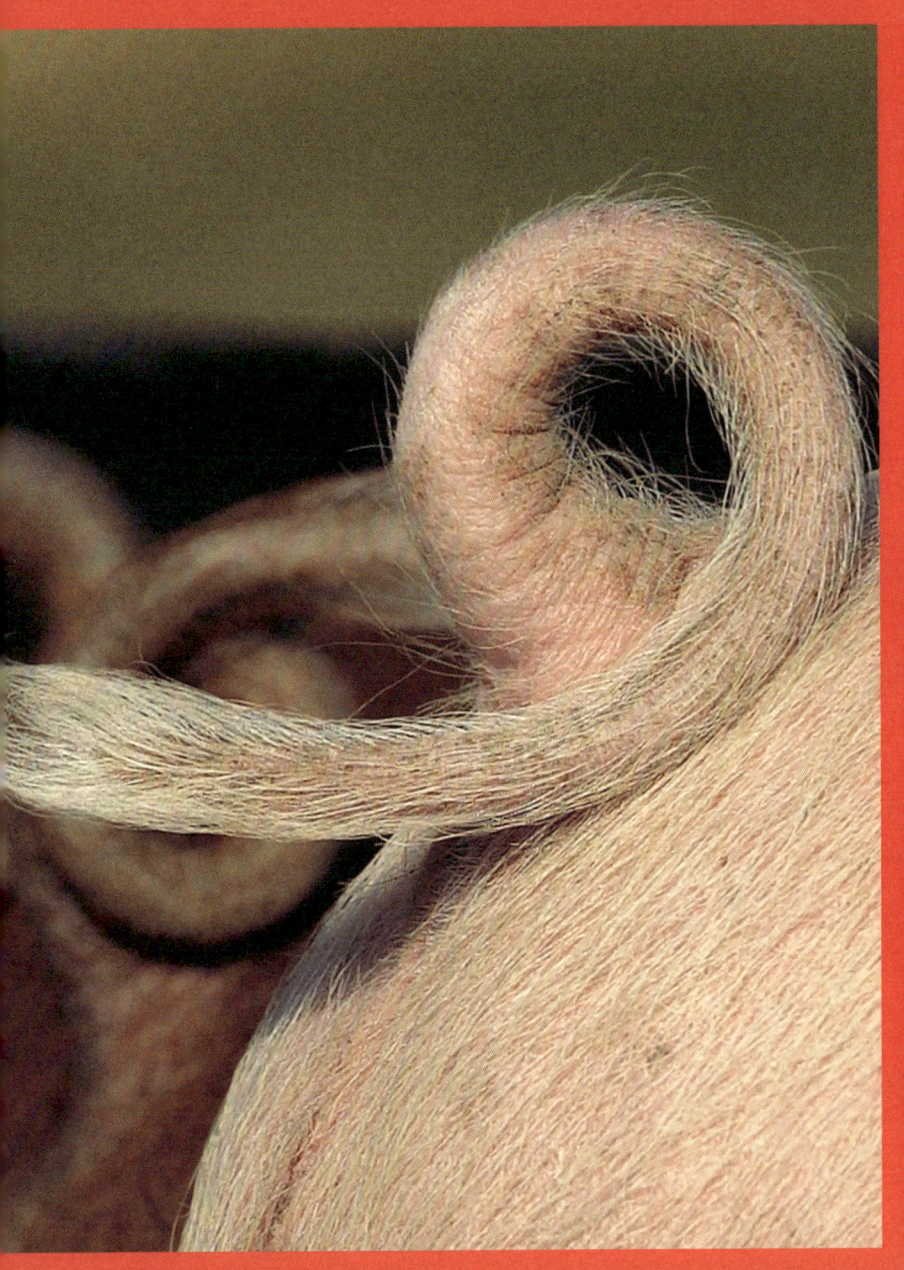

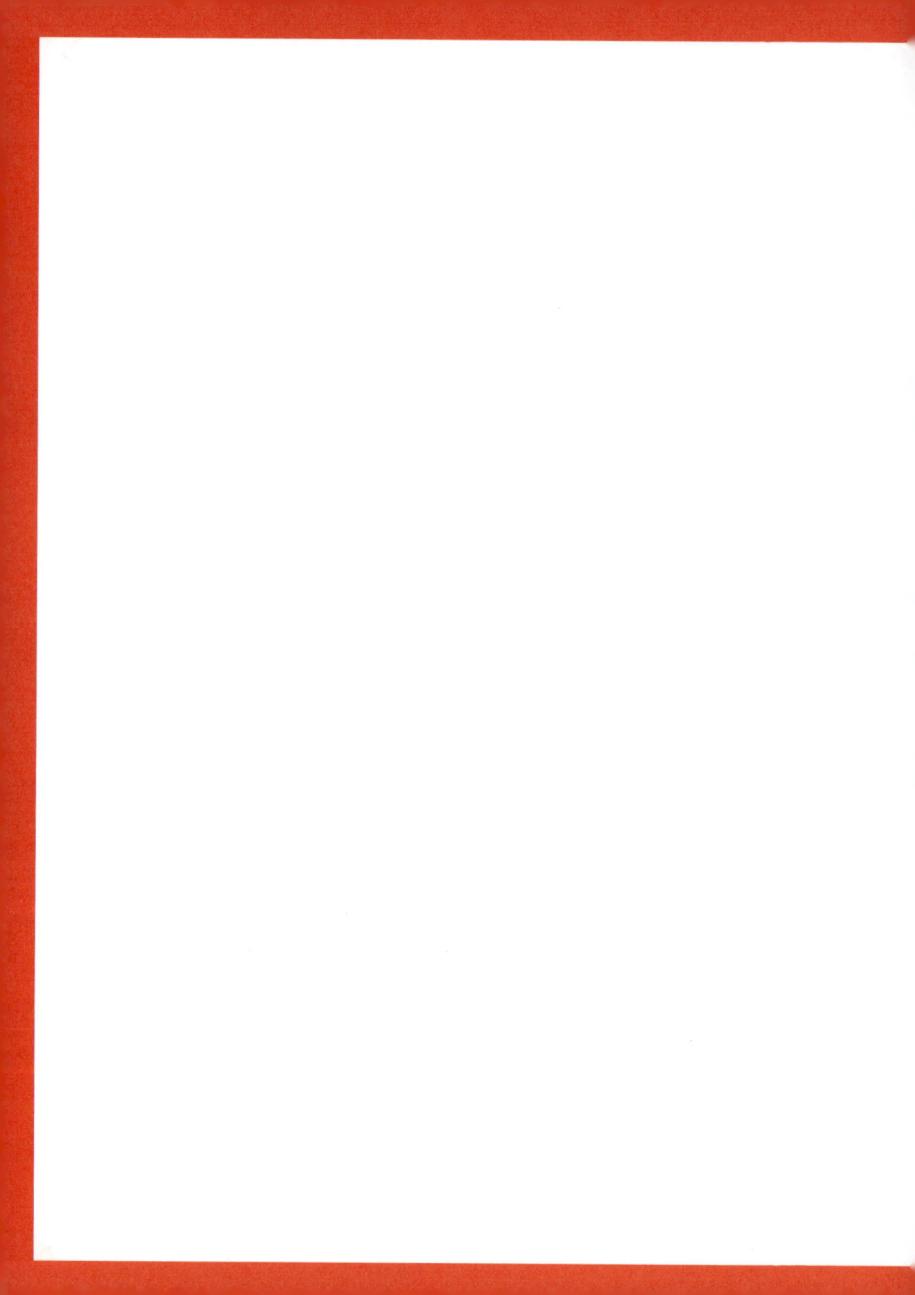

TWINS (1988)

Beetle (2010)

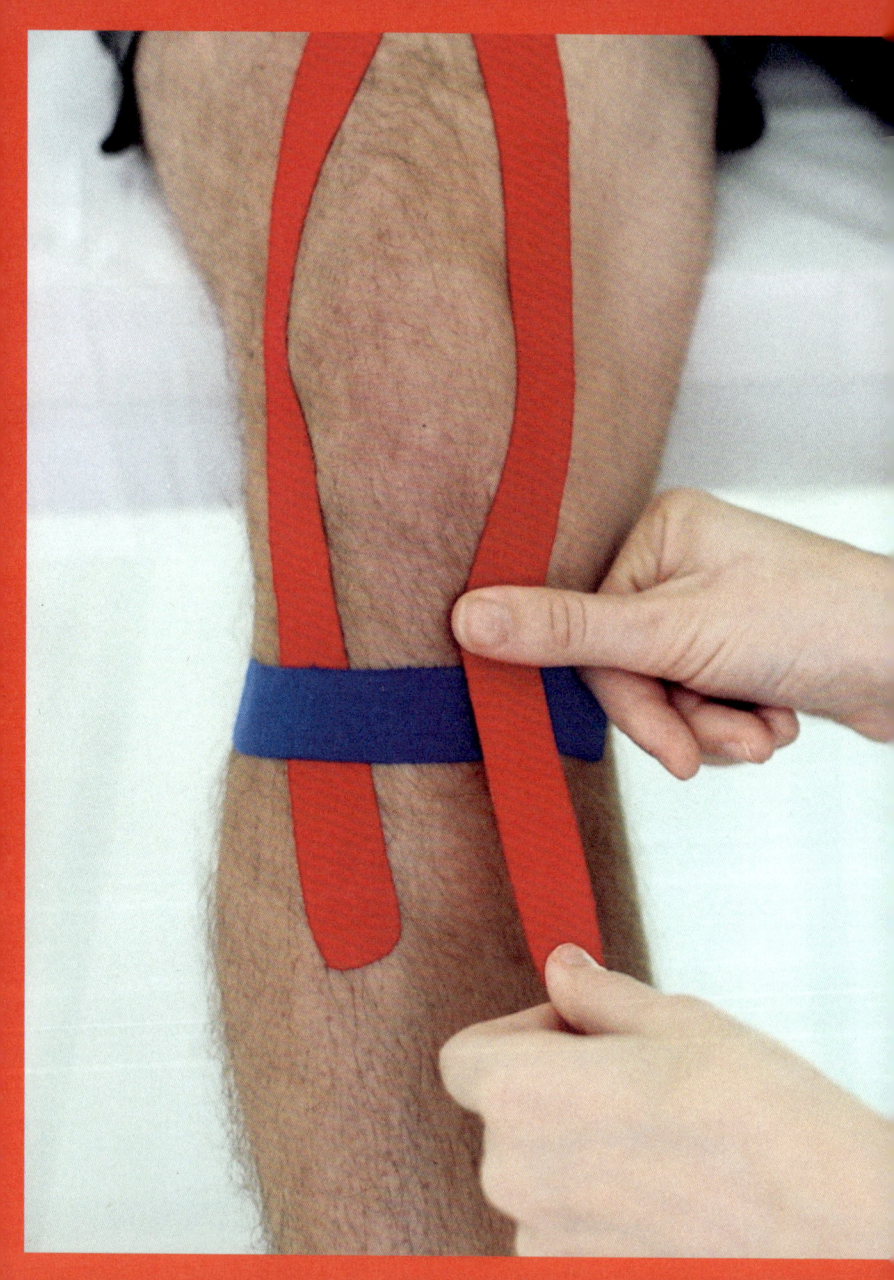

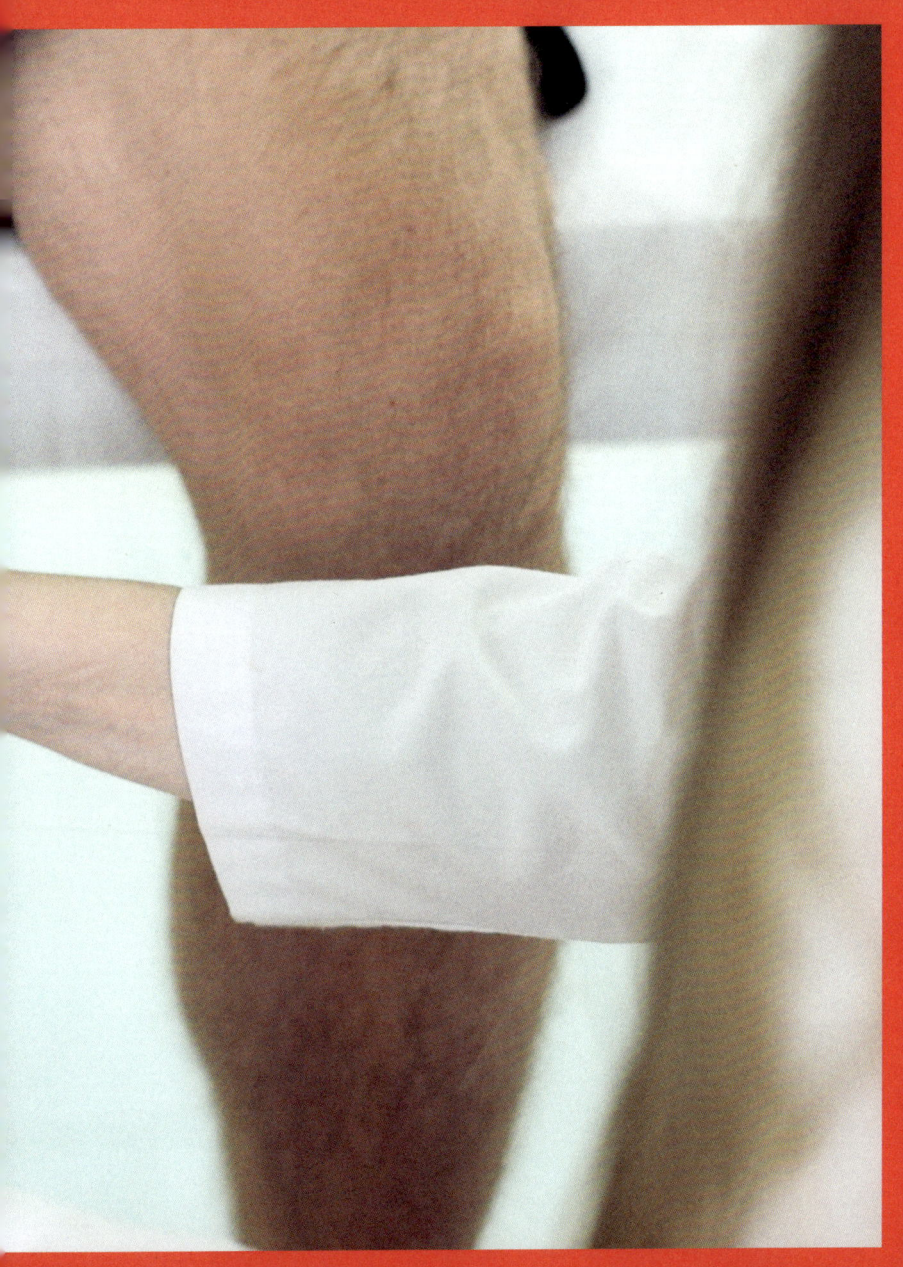

Dub (2016)

Palmera (1985)

Junction (2022)

Wabi (2000)

Nothing (2019)

Runner (1982)

Camper Together with Kiko Kostadinov (2020)

Pelotas Nu (2014)

Mix (1995)

Kobarah (2016)

Camper Together with Bernhard Willhelm (2010)

Lathouma (1998)

Camaleón (1975)

Due to copyright, the image on this spread cannot be shown. Please read the description.

The image depicts a professional tennis match being played on a grass court, likely at a renowned tournament such as Wimbledon, given the distinct design of the court and stands. The stadium is crowded with spectators in tiered seating, creating an energetic atmosphere. The players are in action on the court, with a net dividing the playing field. Officials, photographers, and ball kids are positioned around the court, and a scoreboard is visible in the background displaying match details. The venue is well-lit and features a traditional design, emphasizing the prestigious nature of the event.

Image description generated by ChatGPT.

Runner Tenis (1999)

Locus BCN (2006)

Teix (1997)

TWINS (1994)

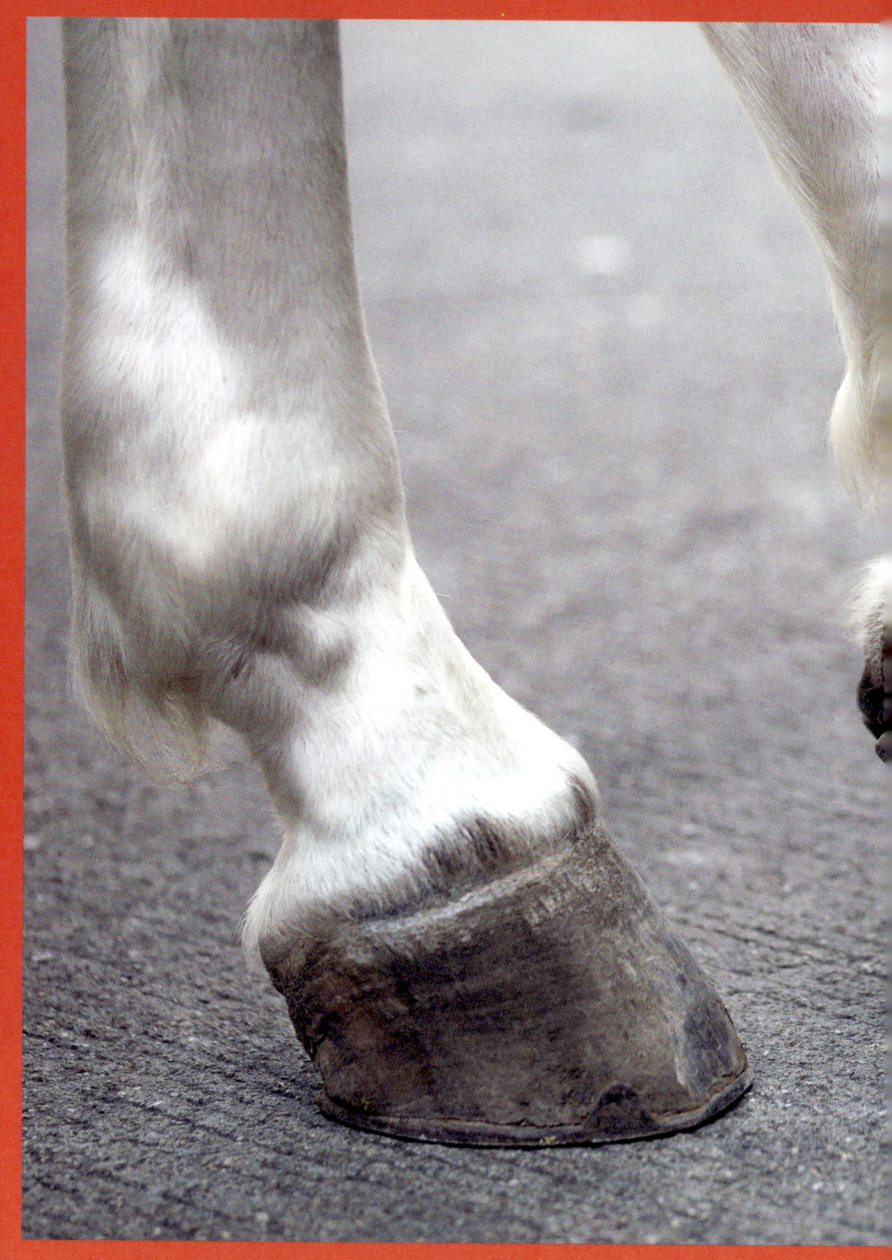

Comic (1998)

Industrial (1989)

ROKU (2023)

Tossu by CAMPERLAB (2022)

Camaleón (1975)

Mix (1995)

Mateo (2016)

Aqua (2001)

Spurn (1998)

TWINS (1988)

Image Credits

 Bence Mate – naturepl.com

 Jarun Tedjaem – Shutterstock.com

 Tui De Roy – naturepl.com

 Sergi Vargas Amengual – Wirestock Creators – stock.adobe.com

 Johannes Liedtke, used under CC BT 4.0. Cropped and modified from original.

 JEHunter – Shutterstock.com

 Scan the QR code

 Doug Lambert – Shutterstock.com

 BlueOrange Studio – Shutterstock.com

 Paul Starosta – Getty Images

 Jennifer – stock.adobe.com

 Konrad Wothe – Minden Pictures

 Jurgens Potgieter – Shutterstock.com

 "Oophaga lehmanni" by Roger Franco Molina, used under CC BY 4.0. Cropped and modified from original.

 Udo Kieslich – stock.adobe.com

 Klein&Hubert – naturepl.com

 ketu_ee – Getty Images

 Dave Denby – Shutterstock.com

 Julia Redl-Freigang – Shutterstock.com

 Ken Griffiths – Shutterstock.com

 "Dromedar-Fuss" by Masteraah, used under CC BY-SA 2.0 DE. Cropped and modified from original.

 Ed van der Elsken – Nederlands Fotomuseum

 fotografixx – Getty Images

 Scan the QR code

 Katesalin Pagkaihang – Shutterstock.com

 Lewkmiller – Getty Images

 Dimitri Otis – Getty Images

 Angela Meier – Shutterstock.com

 Scan the QR code

 Sean Pavone – Shutterstock.com

 "Walk of the People NY 1984" by Bgbg4444, used under CC BY-SA 4.0. Cropped and modified from original.

 "Mobilus In Mobili", CC BY-SA 2.0, via Wikimedia Commons. Cropped and modified from original.

 Scan the QR code

 Per Grunditz – Shutterstock.com

 Scan the QR code

 Untitled Title – Shutterstock.com

 Oleg Yakovlev – Shutterstock.com

 Matyas Rehak – Shutterstock.com

 NASA – earthobservatory.nasa.gov/features/NightLights

 Entertainment Pictures – Alamy

 Scan the QR code

 Roland Seitre – naturepl.com

 Scan the QR code

 Emanuele Biggi – naturepl.com

 Andrew V Marcus – Shutterstock.com

 Jens Schlueter – Getty Images

 "A group of Hindu monks walking their way to the Kumbh Mela 2013" by Seba Della and Sole Bossio, used under CC BY 2.0. Cropped and modified from original.

 imageBROKER – stock.adobe.com

 Pasqua Giacomo – Shutterstock.com

 Frederik Pesch

 Jon Alkain – Shutterstock.com

 TJ Rich – naturepl.com

 Alessandro Manco – Getty Images

 Scan the QR code

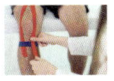 H_Ko – Shutterstock.com

 Michael Fitzsimmons – Shutterstock.com

 Nestor Rizhniak – Shutterstock.com

 Image Broker on Of... – Shutterstock.com

 Wagner Vilas – Shutterstock.com

 Kaiskynet Studio – Shutterstock.com

 Gerard Soury – Getty Images

 Zeljko Radojko – Shutterstock.com

 Naturfoto Honal – Getty Images

 Yulia Raneva – Shutterstock.com

 Hello Lovely – Alamy

 Munimara – Shutterstock.com

 noomcpk – Shutterstock.com

 Da-kuk – Getty Images

 Igor Stevanovic – Alamy

 Equigini – Getty Images

 Nadezda Murmakova – Shutterstock.com

 Pamela Weston – Shutterstock.com

 A'Studio – Shutterstock.com

 nutty45934 – Shutterstock.com

 Pavel1964 – Shutterstock.com

 Peter Lane – Alamy

 CFimages – Alamy

 Noa Novoa – Shutterstock.com

© 2025, Camper, authors and Verlag der Buchhandlung Walther und Franz König, Köln

All rights reserved. This book may not be reproduced in whole or in part, in any form without written permission from the publisher

Editors
Irma Boom, Frederik Pesch, Camper Design Team

Text
Camper

Image Descriptions
Chat GPT

Project Management
Camper

Design
Irma Boom, Frederik Pesch

Copy Editing & Proofreading
Camper

Printing & Binding
Wilco Art Books, Amersfoort

First published by
Verlag der Buchhandlung Walther und Franz König
Ehrenstraße 4, D–50672 Köln

Bibliographic information published by the Deutsche Nationalbibliothek The Deutsche Nationalbibliothek lists this publication in the Deutsche Nationalbibliografie; detailed bibliographic data are available in the Internet at http://dnb.d-nb.de.

Printed in the Netherlands

Distribution

Europe
Buchhandlung Walther König
Ehrenstraße 4
D – 50672 Köln
+49 (0) 221 / 20 59 6 53
verlag@buchhandlung-walther-koenig.de

UK & Ireland
Art Data
12 Bell Industrial Estate
50 Cunnington Street
London W4 5HB
United Kingdom
+44 (0)208 747 10 61
+44 (0)208 742 23 19
orders@artdata.co.uk

Outside Europe
D.A.P. / Distributed Art Publishers, Inc.
75 Broad Street, Suite 630
USA – New York, NY 10004
+1 (0) 212 627 1999
orders@dapinc.com

ISBN 978-3-7533-0789-3
DL PM 00832-2024

Published in celebration of Camper's 50th anniversary.